IRONPLANNER

Iron-Distance Organizer for Triathletes

Download and customize your own worksheets:

The worksheets, checklists and logs in Ironplanner are available for download at: www.m-m-sports.com/extras/ironplanner (Password: HSEpNAbkq4) or www.Ironplannerworksheets.net
Put them in a binder along with race-related documents, inspirational photos, training plan and important notes so everything is in one place.

Ironman Edition

IRONPLANNER

IRON-DISTANCE ORGANIZER
FOR TRIATHLETES

by Ingrid Loos Miller

Meyer & Meyer Sport

IRONMAN® is a registered trademark of World Triathlon Corporation

British Library Cataloguing in Publication Data
A catalogue record for this book is available from the British Library

Ingrid Loos Miller, Ironplanner
Maidenhead: Meyer & Meyer Sport (UK) Ltd., 2009
ISBN 978-1-84126-257-4

© 2009 by Meyer & Meyer Sport (UK) Ltd.
Aachen, Adelaide, Auckland, Budapest, Cape Town, Graz, Indianpolis,
Maidenhead, New York, Olten (CH), Singapore, Toronto
Member of the World
Sport Publishers' Association (WSPA)
www.w-s-p-a.org
Printed and bound by: B.O.S.S Druck und Medien GmbH, Germany
ISBN 978-1-84126-257-4
E-Mail: verlag@m-m-sports.com
www.m-m-sports.com

Contents

ACKNOWLEDGMENTS

I wish to thank my husband Chris. He is the most persistent man I know and the face I long to see at the finish line. He endures my athletic enthusiasms with grace. I also thank many others including my dad Henk Loos who knows well the nuance of peak performance and singular focus, and my mom Jansje Loos, who like a tiger, has been quietly and athletically moving each day for the last 30 years. My brother Charles Loos helped me get started with writing for magazines years ago and I still use the books he sent me.

Thomas Stengel and Meyer & Meyer Publishing embraced this unique project and I appreciate their confidence in me. My physical therapist/ coach Jim Herkimer (SportsConditioningAndRehabilitation.com) made me strong, kept me injury-free and encouraged my obsession with keeping track of things. Fellow Ironmen Tim Harward and Kurt Adams provided thoughtful criticism. Dale Ghere freed me to write when I was tied in knots. Christine Fugate helped me to call myself "a writer". Joe Talavera constantly reminds me what passion for racing is. Sue Ellen Miller knows how unpredictable life is, and inspired me to jump into the pool with both feet before all the water is gone.

The World Triathlon Corporation took a hair-brained dare and created from it a race that tickles the imagination of thousands and thousands more each year; the dream of becoming an Ironman. For that there can not be thanks enough.

INTRODUCTION

DON'T DO AN IRONMAN WITHOUT AN IRONPLANNER

The inspiration for this book came from my own Ironman journey. Every week I wondered why it seemed that every waking moment was spent doing something related to the Ironman, even when I was not training.

There was no end to the information available; my problem was managing it all. I did not need another training log, what I needed was an organizer with lists of the plethora of details I had to attend to. I needed an Ironplanner so I made one.

In bringing this to you, Ironman hopeful or veteran, I hope to save you some time-time you will need to rest, work, or be with your family during your journey.

Doing an Ironman is a big deal. You need a big plan. Here it is and happy racing.

1

IRON-DISTANCE FAQ'S

WHAT IS IT LIKE TO TRAIN FOR AN IRONMAN?

THE SACRIFICES...

Ironman training is a job. Twenty hours of training time translates to 30 hours when you include the time spent getting dressed for, getting to and from workouts, planning for the various aspects of the race, and laying flat on your bed waiting for the world to stop spinning. The time you need to prepare mentally for the event is rarely discussed, but it should be. Even when you are doing other things like going to work or being a mom, you function in a semi-zombie state of fatigue, both mentally and physically.

This will not be the time to take-on anything extra at work. Lunchtime will be training time, and overtime can unravel your training plan. Training in the dark will be unavoidable. You can manage intellectual tasks in the morning, but the afternoon slump will be worse than usual.

Aside from obligations at work, every activity must be evaluated in terms of whether it will interfere with training and recovery time. Your social universe shrinks by necessity and by choice. Being around large groups of people increases the chance of illness so limiting your social calendar will help you stay healthy.

You will not be able to make many deposits into the bank of goodwill with your spouse. This is the time when you will be doing more taking than giving. Getting to bed early is required and it may mean going to bed alone. The late night television program you are addicted to will have to go on without you for a season.

If you are used to doing the cooking, you will have to change that too. Standing up at the kitchen counter preparing food for an hour a day will put you over the edge of fatigue, not to mention the time spent planning meals, shopping and cleaning up after them. Convenience foods will take center stage. Bagged salads, soups, frozen items, and pre-made meals are the only way to feed yourself and your brood. Most of your time in the kitchen will be spent mixing fuel and recovery potions.

Even though you are spending many hours training, you will be quite sloth-like the rest of the time. No more walking to the local corner store. Sometimes it is a struggle to walk to the mailbox.

When you need to shop, there isn't time or energy to drive around town looking for the best deal. The internet will be your best friend for shopping. Your UPS and FEDEX guy will be regular visitors.

As a parent, you will not be able to volunteer to help at school. The PTA is out. If you can keep your kids healthy, fed and getting most of their homework done, congratulate yourself. You will not be able to take your kids to sports activities on a regular basis. They will have less of your focus and energy for the duration of your training.

THE PAYOFF...

But it isn't all bad. In fact, training for an Ironman is the most exhilarating experience you may ever have. The fatigue and the looming challenge sharpen your senses and carry you through on an endorphin high like no other. You feel intensely alive, marveling at the wondrous machine that is your body. Day after day the movements of swimming, cycling and running are refined to bring you to the finish line on the best day of your life.

The singular focus is where real life ends and the allure of Ironman begins. It guarantees escape to the remote regions of your imagination, to that place where your dreams live, where you hold visions of great triathletes and wishes for the kind of competitor you hope to be. To truly take flight in training, you have to let your mind go to that place that transcends the limitations of genetics, age, your body type and your bulges. You *become* Mark Allen or Natascha Badmann. You become Chrissie Wellington or Craig Alexander or that unnamed super fit triathlete that zooms by you on the bike. You know the one.

Your body will change for the better. Enjoy it. Your spouse will enjoy it to. You will be able to eat—no, you will *need* to eat—everything in sight. Unless you have an enormous stomach, you have to indulge in calorie-dense food to meet your caloric needs.

The singular experience of training for and completing an Ironman changes your life because at its core, it changes how you see yourself. No matter who you are when you start, you will be fitter, stronger, more disciplined, more powerful in every aspect of your life when you finish. You will be just a little bit ... invincible.

CAN I DO THIS?

Other than, "Can I finish?", the most common question from Ironman hopefuls is, "Can I train and keep my job and my family intact?" If you have a reasonable training plan, your family supports you, your boss is willing to give you some extra time off and doesn't expect overtime then, yes, you can fit the training in. Whether you will finish or not is the question only you can answer. Timing is crucial, as discussed below. There are many ifs, but there always are.

Realize that by undertaking the Ironman, you will be sacrificing something else. The time spent preparing for an Ironman is enough to write a novel, to add a room to the house, or to start a new career.

WHAT ABOUT TIME LIMITS?

To be an Ironman, you must swim 2.4 miles, bike 112 miles and run 26.2 miles in no more than 17 hours. If you are still running when the time limit expires, you will probably be able to finish your race, but you will not be an official finisher. That means no medal, no T-shirt, and no one to say "you are an Ironman!" as you cross the finish line.

It is the time limit that makes this race so compelling and such a challenge. There is no point entering in Ironman if you have no chance of making the time limit.

The best way to prevent a disappointment like that is to make sure you can make the cut-off times by doing each distance as a stand alone, well within the allotted time. If you can do each event alone in a total of less than 17 hours you are good to go, but realize that your times may be slower on race day because it will combine all 3 events.

There are also time limits for each event. They vary a little but the World Championship Ironman cut-off time is the standard. The swim must be completed 2:20 after the start of the race. The bike ride must be completed 10:30 after the start, and the Run, 17:00. There are sometimes additional cut-off times. I can think of little worse than training your heart out for 6 months, only to be pulled from the course because you missed a time cut-off.

It can take a year or two to get each of these distances under your belt. It is time well spent. The journey to Ironman can be a long one.

WHEN SHOULD I DO IT?

Timing is important. Your body and mind have to be ready for the rigors of training, the race has to fit your schedule, and you have to find one that you can enter.

Getting into a race is a challenge in itself. Most of them fill up a year in advance. Many of them fill the day after the race and you have to travel there and stand in line to get a spot for the following year. International races fill more slowly, but carry a hefty price tag in travel expenses. Other races of the same distance that do not carry the "Ironman" title are considerably easier to enter, but they usually draw smaller crowds and less support, so consider it carefully.

Once you decide to do an Ironman, the actual race day could be 2 years away. It may take a year or more to accomplish the preliminary goals that will make you ready to begin your Ironman training.

It is best to approach an Ironman in steps:

1. You need at least 2 years of endurance racing experience. It will be 3 by the time you get to the starting line at your Ironman race.

2. Do the race distance in each discipline; a 2.4 mile swim (69 lengths of a 25-yard pool), a 112 mile bike ride and a 26.2 mile run well within Ironman time limits.

Each of these tasks requires an investment in time and training but if you can't do each component alone, you have no business trying to combine them into a single day.

3. Combine some of the disciplines in a single long race. Aqua bike races combine the 2.4 mile swim with the 112 mile bike. If you can't find one of those, try a half-Ironman distance race. A word of caution though, a 70.3 only resembles an Ironman in the type and order of disciplines. Competitors doing 70.3 attack the course with the fury of a sprint and they don't slow down. You might feel terribly outclassed in a 70.3 yet do well in an Ironman where the attitude is markedly different.

If you still are burning to do an Ironman, find a race that will fit your schedule and your pocketbook. Once you have found your race, it is time to commit. Check the entry requirements. Some races require completion of a half-ironman, or 70.3 distance event within one year. You will need 6 months to train for the event. The bulk of it will be in the last 3 months, so check the calendar. Do not schedule heavy training months during your busy time of year.

All it takes is a point and a click. At that moment your stomach will drop so loudly that the neighbors will hear it-talk about adrenaline. Let the adventure begin.

DO I NEED A COACH?

Hiring a good coach will give you the best chance of getting to the starting line with your body, work and family life intact. Having someone else worry about the details of volume, intensity and periodization will save you a tremendous amount of time. Training plans abound, but it is important to have someone that you can meet with face-to-face.

Internet coaching has its limitations. Internet coaches can't see if you look drawn and pale. An email won't reveal that you are mentally exhausted. At the very least, find someone you can talk to on the phone periodically.

A coach will give you a training plan that you can have confidence in. It will fit your schedule and your limitations – a bad back, muscle cramping problems, a recurring knee injury or a tendency to overdo it in training. You can be confident that your workouts are within your capacity to complete at the speed and intensity required.

It takes some effort to find a coach that you have confidence in. The role of a coach starts with the training plan, but the real value is having someone that helps you build your body and gain confidence in your own ability. The cheerleading aspect of a coach is crucial to optimizing your preparation. Personal rapport is crucial to the success of the relationship.

If you prefer to use a ready-made training plan, use one that starts with training volume (hours) that you can easily handle. There should also be cycles of build-up and recovery time. See *The Triathlete's Training Bible* by Joe Friel for the last word in formulating a training plan.

If you don't have a coach, be extra vigilant with your record keeping so that when a little injury occurs, you can give a detailed history to your physical therapist. Ironman training will test your limits and you will likely need professional medical help at some point with some kind of issue.

WHO DO I NEED?

Even if you plan to train solo, you can't do an Ironman alone.

- Coach/personal trainer/advisor you can meet with personally

- Physical therapist that works with athletes

- Massage therapist

- Friends to cheer you on

- Other athletes to train with at times

- Family to love you no matter what and to pick up the slack because you are too busy or tired to contribute

- Babysitter

- Bike mechanic

- The internet universe for blogs, race reports, supplies and advice

- Caretaker for your pets when you travel to the race

WHAT DO I NEED?

You need the same equipment you already have for shorter distance triathlons, just more of it and in greater variety to handle training in every kind of weather and for longer periods of time. See Chapter 11 for Special Clothing Considerations.

A heart rate monitor is crucial for monitoring your exertion. Controlling exertion is the single most important factor within your control on race day. If you don't have one, get one. Your coach or training plan will tell you how to use it.

WHAT WILL IT COST?

This depends on how much you have to buy. Let's assume that you are well-equipped for short-distance races. Some of the items on this list are for things you would normally use even if you are not doing an Ironman. It will be more if you have to travel by air. Here is a rundown of costs:

- Entry fee $500

- Hotel for 3 nights (single occupant) $500

- Meals at race venue for 3 days $200

- Coaching for 6 months, usually about $200 per month, $1200

- Fueling drinks, gels, bars $350 ($1 per serving and one-half serving per training hour)

- Recovery protein shakes $300

- Replacement strap for heart rate monitor $60

- Adjust bike fit to more aero position $60

- Pre-race bike tune-up $150

- New tires, extra tubes and air for bike $150

- Clothing including swim suits, caps, bike shorts and shirts, tights, gloves, compression shorts, running tops $300

- 2-pair swim goggles $60

- Pool fees $300

- Gym fees (included in coaching)

- Physical therapy $180

- Books, magazines, DVDs $140

- Running shoes $100

- Race souvenirs $200

Grand Total: $4400

Iron-distance racing is not cheap, but it is worth it.

Suggested Reading:
Going Long: Training for Ironman-Distance Triathlons, Joe Friel and Gordon Byrn, Velopress 2003
The Triathlete's Training Bible, Second Edition, Joe Friel, Velopress 2004

IRONPLANNER COUNTDOWN

HOW TO USE THIS BOOK

Training for an Ironman takes 6 months. At the beginning it seems like the race is far away and all you can think about is the training. But those months are also filled with organizational challenges that are best managed along the way rather than a few weeks before the race. The better organized you are, the more you will get from your efforts.

Ironplanner is full of checklists and worksheets that will help you plan, organize and manage your Ironman preparation. To get the greatest benefit from this book, you should work through all of the material. You can download the worksheets from www.m-m-sports.com/extras/ironplanner or www.Ironplannerworksheets.net and put them into a binder, folder or up on your wall. Physical Training, coupled with the components addressed in your Ironplanner will bring Ironman success.

It all starts with the Ironplanner Countdown, a master list of everything you have to do to get you to the starting line. Many of the elements addressed in the Ironplanner will go into your Race Plan (see Fig.1)

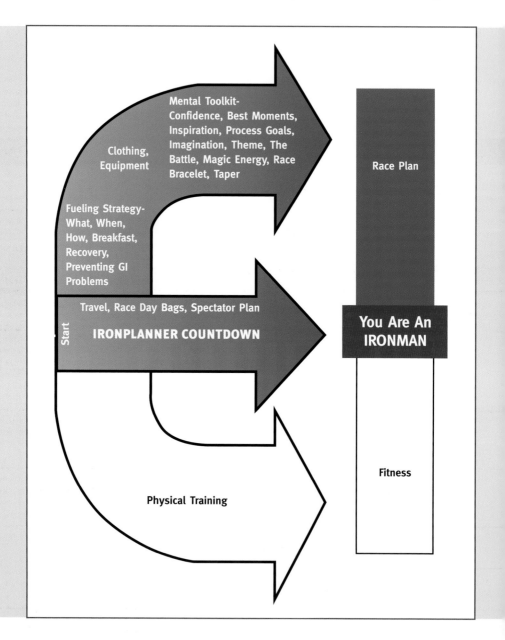

Figure 1 *Darkened areas are addressed in Ironplanner*

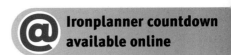
Everything on the Ironplanner countdown is discussed in this book. References to particular worksheets are in italic. Some of these tasks can be completed in a few minutes, but many of them, like finding a training plan or coach, may take days or weeks. Draw a line through the items as they are completed.

GETTING STARTED

To Do ASAP

1	Enter race. Write the date on your calendar.
2	Make a folder for important Ironman documents.
3	Print race entry and put it in document folder.
4	Find out when race check-in is so you can make travel plans.
5	Review race course to find good hotel location.
6	Tell friends and family about the race.
7	Create a contingency plan. What will you do if you are unable to race your Ironman?
8	Make travel and hotel reservations. Record in *Travel Worksheet*, Chapter 7.
9	Print all travel reservations and put them into document folder.
10	Find a training plan/coach. See Chapter 1.
11	Determine heart rate based training zones as instructed by your coach or training plan.

THE FIRST 3 MONTHS

12	Find 2 different swimming facilities. Write hours/fee/contact number in *Contacts and Facilities Appendix*.
13	Start *Race Resume* in Chapter 4.
14	Study the swim course. Use it to *Imagine Being There* and *Slice It Up*, Chapter 4.
15	Study the race course for Bike leg. Use it to *Imagine Being There* and *Slice It Up*, Chapter 4.
16	Study the race course for Run. Use it to *Imagine Being There* and *Slice It Up*, Chapter 4.
17	Make sure you have a wetsuit, goggles, swim gear.
18	Make sure you have bike shoes, helmet, sunglasses, gloves, bike tools and tubes.
19	Find a measured running area/track for intervals.
20	Find riding routes and make contingency plan for bad weather- gym/trainer?
21	Confirm all hotel and travel reservations. See *Travel Worksheet*, Chapter 7.

ONGOING TASKS

The items do be done on an ongoing basis should be reviewed regularly. Review this list during the recovery week of each training cycle. For the most part, the tasks will not be completed until you write your race plan. Continue to refine your Race Plan up to a few days before the race.

	To Do Regularly Throughout Training
22	Create fueling plan for bike leg. Experiment with what to carry and how to carry it on your bike. See Chapter 6.
23	Make/update plans/goals for post-race. Write them in *Post Race Worksheet*, Chapter 10.
24	Add mantras to *Mantras Worksheet*, Chapter 5.
25	Practice imagining the swim with your *Race Visualization Checklist*, Chapter 5.
26	Practice imagining the bike leg with your *Race Visualization Checklist*, Chapter 5.
27	Practice imagining the run with your *Race Visualization Checklist*, Chapter 5.
28	Add to *Inspiration List*, Chapter 5.
29	Practice shifting focus inward, then outward during long bike ride. See Chapter 5.
30	Practice mile-by-mile focus during long run.
31	During a long swim remember 3 best moments from your past. Record in *Best Moments Worksheet*, Chapter 5.

32	During a long ride remember 3 best moments from your past. Record in *Best Moments Worksheet*, Chapter 5.
33	During a long run, remember 3 best moments from your past. Record in *Best Moments Worksheet*, Chapter 5.
34	During a long bike ride, think of mantras that improve your form. Record in *Mantras Worksheet*, Chapter 5.
35	During a long run, think of mantras that improve your form. Record in *Mantras Worksheet*, Chapter 5.
36	During a long swim, think of mantras that improve your form. Record in *Mantras Worksheet*, Chapter 5.
37	Experiment with race day clothing.
38	Update *Fueling Worksheets* in Chapter 6. Try different fueling products if necessary.
39	Experiment with breakfasts to eat on race day. Update *Fueling Worksheets*, Chapter 6.
40	Read everything you can find about your race. Use these details to *Imagine Being There*, Chapter 4.
41	Create a new process goal for each leg of the race. Record in *Process Goals Worksheet*, Chapter 5.
42	Record your *Best Moments* in training. See Chapter 5.
43	Experiment with fuels supplied at race.
44	Decide and record what to pack in race day bags, Chapter 8.
45	Make packing list of non-racing items for race.

THE FINAL 3 MONTHS

46	Adjust bike fit to be more aero if needed.
47	Arrange for bike transport to race venue. Record in *Travel Worksheet*, Chapter 7.
48	Plan some low energy/low risk activities for taper weeks.
49	Imagine *The Battle* and draw it on worksheet in Chapter 5.
50	Imagine a Magic energy source when you are tired during training. Record it in your *Make Magic worksheet*, Chapter 5.
51	Set all of your watches, monitors and computers with planned time (feeding, walk-run, heart rate zones). See Chapter 5.
52	Write at least 3 process goals for bike leg. Record in *Race Plan*, Chapter 9
53	Write at least 3 process goals for run leg. Record in *Race Plan*, Chapter 9
54	Buy and put aside fuel power/gels, etc for race day.
55	Practice changing a bike tire in the middle of a long ride.
56	Will your running shoes make it through race day? Buy new ones now so they are broken in by race day.

THE FINAL MONTH

The last month before the race is full of anticipation. All of the training hours are tucked safely away and all you have to do is avoid injury.

To Do One Month Prior To Race

57	Review all that you have written in your Ironplanner worksheets and lists. Decide what to incorporate into your *Race Plan*, Chapter 9.
58	Find activities for family at race venue. Put information in document folder.
59	Develop "expected" and "dream" times based on training and conditions. Record in *Time Prediction Worksheet*, *Race Plan* and *Spectator Plan*. See Chapter 9.
60	Create a theme for each discipline. Record in *Race Plan*. See Chapter 5.
61	Update your Race Resume and be impressed with all you have accomplished. See Chapter 4.
62	Do a long swim in your wetsuit. Where will you put anti-chaffing lotion? How long does it take to put the wetsuit on properly? Where are the seams?
63	Plan calming strategy for race morning. Record in *Race Plan*. Chapter 9.
64	Arrange for pet care during absence at race. Record in *Contacts and Facilities Appendix*.
65	Create a plan for each transition. Include in *Race Plan*, Chapter 9.
66	Finalize mental plan for each discipline. Include in *Race Plan*, Chapter 9.

To Do In Final Month Before Race

67	Finalize and record what to pack in *Race Day Bags*, Chapter 8.
68	Print driving directions to hotel, put them in document file.
69	Review mental strategy for a meltdown, just in case. See Chapter 5.
70	Study the race course for the Swim. *Imagine Being There* and *Slice it Up*, Chapter 4. Record in *Race Plan*, Chapter 9.
71	Make detailed plan for 1 week pre-race. Add it to Ironplanner Countdown as needed.
72	Review detailed *Race Plan* for each discipline. See Chapter 9.
73	Review the race rules in their entirety, especially the information on time penalties.
74	Have bike tuned-up and checked by mechanic.

To Do 2 Weeks Before Race

75	Buy/obtain items to be placed in special needs bags. See Chapter 8.
76	Make mental strategy notes/race bracelet to have with you on race day. See Chapter 5.
77	Prepare spectator information packets for friends/family, Chapter 7.
78	Revisit your *Time Prediction Worksheet* and make copies for your friends and family. See Chapter 9.
79	Review and print copies of *Race Information* from race website and include in spectator packets.

RACE WEEK

The final week before the race is hectic. The sooner you start your packing, the better. This is also when you may start to have strange dreams. Rest up as much as possible and remain cautious about large crowds and home improvement projects.

By now you have filled in all of the blanks in your Ironplanner. All that is left is to pack and get to the race venue, and let your masterful plan unfold.

	To Do The Week Before The Race
80	Shop for food and last minute items. Do you need reflective tape? Do you need electrical tape to mount your gels on your bike?
81	Review race plan in detail.
82	Check weather forecast for race venue daily. Adjust race plan as needed.
83	Review race rules regarding time penalties.
84	Check that cleats are tight before packing your shoes.
85	Bring bike to shipper/transport company.
86	Re-confirm all hotel and travel reservations.
87	Start packing equipment and non-perishables-Don't forget your Ironplanner and document folder.
88	Pack/Make ready race clothes for possible weather conditions. Make final clothing decision on race day.
89	Plan menu for day before the race.

AT THE RACE VENUE

By the time you get to the race venue, the fact that you are going to race will be very real indeed. Enjoy the camaraderie with the other athletes and try to keep your stress level down. Be good to your legs, don't stand or walk more than you need to.

To Do 2 Days Before The Race

90	Registration and packet pick-up. Make sure you have a timing chip.
91	Plan your transportation to race venue on race day. How will your family get there?
92	Transfer packed items into *Race Day Bags*.
93	Purchase last-minute items needed for race.
94	Tour the race course.
95	Visit Vendors at Expo.
96	Attend Pre-Race Athlete meeting.
97	Pick-up bike from transport service.
98	Practice swim on race course. Decide whether neoprene cap is needed.
99	Eat according to your plan.
100	Review your race plan.
101	Visit the transition area, swim start and transition ins and outs.
102	Hang your wetsuit to dry after the practice swim so it is dry on race day.

The day before the race is your opportunity to gather your thoughts and steel yourself for the effort of the race. Rest as much as possible.

	To Do The Day Before The Race
103	Do anything still left on list above.
104	Double check contents of race day bags before dropping them off.
105	Decide what you will load onto your bike before dropping it off & what you will bring with you in the morning.
106	Check your bike for malfunctions, flats, repair as needed. Make sure it is in an easy gear before you rack it.
107	Check the various watches, monitors and computers. Are they set correctly for the race?
108	Make plans for bike and bag pick-up after the race.
109	Drop bike and race day bags at race venue if required.
110	Eat according to your plan.
111	Spend a few hours alone relaxing and preparing mentally for the race-what will your family do during this time?
112	Stay off your feet as much as possible.
113	Decide what time to wake-up. Set 2 alarms and request wake-up call.
114	Lay out clothing and what to bring with you the next day.
115	Make sure someone will be at the finish with your finish line bag.

To Do The Day Before The Race

116	Finalize your transportation to the race venue.
117	Go to bed early. Even if you don't sleep, rest.
118	Review your race plan.
119	Make final decision on clothing based on expected weather conditions.

To Do In The Morning On Race Day

120	Wake-up, get dressed, and eat.
121	Apply first layer of sunscreen, below eyes only.
122	Put on your timing chip, watch, monitor, chest strap.
123	Bring Race Bag #1 (dry clothes).
124	Know that this will be a wonderful day and by midnight it will all be over.

To Do On Race Day At Venue

125	Make sure you are wearing your timing chip.
126	Load Fuel on your bike as planned.
127	Get into bathroom line even if you don't need to.

To Do On Race Day At Venue

128 Sit as much as possible until it is time to get into the water and start the race.

129 Give yourself ample time to squeeze into your wetsuit.

130 Get in the water and do your swim warm-up.

131 Find a good starting position for the swim. Fast swimmers in front, slower in back or on the side.

132 Follow your *Race Plan*.

133 Take it all in with joyful anticipation.

To Do The Day After The Race

134 Eat. Eat. Eat.

135 Visit vendors for "Finisher" merchandise.

136 Forgive yourself for everything. Rejoice in your accomplishment. You are an Ironman.

TRAINING LOG & SUMMARIES

Training for an Ironman is a monumental task. Training plans are available through coaches, online and in print. The challenge is finding a plan that is realistic for you and your particular limitations.

Use a plan tailored to your experience level, your age and your speed. The starting weekly training volume (hours) should be close to your current level. Training plans should also build in cycles, allowing recovery weeks and rest days.

It will take about 6 months to train for your race. It is important to keep track of what you are doing. Marking off workouts as you complete them will save you some time. Mental strategies are discussed in Chapter 4 and 5, and Fueling is in Chapter 6. There are 2 versions of training summary sheets. Both allow you to track your training volume at a glance. Increasing your volume too quickly is a likely cause of injury so these summaries will show quickly if you are headed for trouble.

If your coach or training plan requires additional details, a Daily Training Log form is provided. Make copies as needed.

DAILY TRAINING LOG

Date   **Weather/temp**   **Wt. before & after**   **Resting HR**

_____

Notes _____

_____

_____

_____

Workout #1

swim • bike • run • strength

Intensity/HR _____

Intervals/Duration/Distance/Speed/Specifics _____

_____

_____

_____

Workout #2

swim • bike • run • strength

Intensity/HR _____

Intervals/Duration/Distance/Speed/Specifics _____

_____

_____

_____

SUMMARY OF WEEKLY TRAINING VOLUME

Date	Mon Sun	Tues Mon	Wed Tues	Thur Wed	Fri Thur

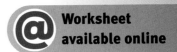
Circle Monday or Sunday start day and record total training time for each day. Also record the longest session in each discipline. Be aware of large jumps in volume that can lead to trouble.

t	Sun Sat	Ttl Hrs	Long Swim	Long Bike	Long Run

SUMMARY OF TRAINING VOLUME BY DISCIPLINE

	Mon Sun	Tues Mon	Wed Tues	Thur Wed
Swim				
Bike				
Run				
Total				
Swim				
Bike				
Run				
Total				
Swim				
Bike				
Run				
Total				
Swim				
Bike				
Run				
Total				
Swim				
Bike				
Run				
Total				
Swim				
Bike				
Run				
Total				

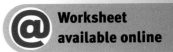
Circle Monday or Sunday start day and record daily and weekly training time in each discipline. Be aware of large jumps in volume that can lead to trouble.

Fri Thur	Sat Fri	Sun Sat	Total hours

4

MENTAL TOOLKIT 1: PRE-RACE

What if you had to prove to someone that you were worthy of this Ironman challenge? Well, you do. You have to prove it to yourself.

You will wait at the starting line with a healthy dose of fear, but it should come from respect for the distance, not from doubts about whether you belong there. You will need confidence to get the most from yourself on race day. But where does it come from?

Self-assurance comes from recognizing your achievements. A Race Resume goes beyond triathlon experience, drawing upon the unique experiences, history and personal attributes you bring to the Ironman table. It will reveal how formidable you *already* are. By the time you are finished training, your body and mind will be primed for the challenge. You will be ready to become an Ironman.

No one else will read it, so write fearlessly. Review and update it often, even after the race. Use the Race Resume Worksheet as a guide.

RACE RESUME WORKSHEET

Name: _____   **Age:** _____

Race Objective: _____

Education:

- Ways in which you have educated yourself about this race: (books, movies, travel, etc.)

Achievements:

- Races, successful training sessions:
- Intermediate goals you have achieved:
- Improvement in fitness levels and physiological markers (reduced % body fat, increased lean body mass, reduced resting HR, increased VO2 max, increased speed at time trials, reduced heart rate for given speed, strength improvements):

Experience:

- Pertinent racing experience: triathlon swim, cycling, running:
- Endurance events you have completed:
- Experiences overcoming adversity:
- Times you have overcome mental adversity to reach a goal:
- Times you have overcome physical adversity and reached a goal:
- Experience with overcoming fear:

Personal Attributes:

- Physical attributes that will help you with this race:
- Personality traits that will help you with this race (persistence, consistent training habits, stubbornness, optimism):
- Particular skills and talents:

Motivation:

- Describe what you will feel when you train for this race:
- Describe what you will feel like when you cross the finish line:
- Describe how it will feel to know you have finished this race:

Support Systems:

- Describe the people (family and professional) that will help you accomplish this goal:

Feasibility:

- Facilities you can use in order to accomplish this goal (gym, pool, etc):
- Equipment you have that will allow you to accomplish this goal:
- Projects you will be able to delay until this goal is achieved:
- Amount of time per week you can devote to pursuing this goal:

Back-up plan:

- What will you do if you are ultimately unable to participate in this race due to accident, illness or other unforeseen circumstance?

RACE RESUME-SAMPLE

Name: *Future Ironman*   **Age:** *40*

Race Objective: *Finish Ironman Race*

Education:
- *I read many books about Ironman distance races.*
- *I have attended clinics on running and swimming.*

Achievements:
- *Ironman 70.3,5 marathons, 3 sprint tri's finishing in the top half of my age group, consistently training for last 2 years.*
- *Swim speed improved from 2:15 per 100 to 2:00 this year.*
- *Body fat reduced by 3% in last 6 months.*

Experience:
- *My races are always exercises in overcoming hardship. I bonked on the run at my 70.3, refueled and recovered. I never miss a workout. I got myself out of debt last year with mental discipline.*
- *I swam the Alcatraz race even though I'm scared of sharks. I survived.*

Personal Attributes:
- *No current physical limitations/injuries. I respond quickly to endurance training. I have strong legs and good core strength.*

- *Stubborn. Focused. Patient. I am better at endurance events than sprints. Good cyclist.*

Motivation:

- *Finishing an Ironman would be a great achievement. Just thinking about it gives me goose bumps. It would be the hardest, greatest thing I ever did athletically.*

Support Systems:

- *My wife thinks I'm a nut but she is very supportive and a great cook. Flexible boss and work schedule.*

Feasibility:

- *I can use the pool at the gym which also has spin bikes and treadmills in case of bad weather.*
- *I already own everything I will need for this race.*
- *Work is flexible and I have no large projects planned. I can devote up to 20 hours per week to training.*

Back-up plan:

- *Oceanside 70.3. I will probably do the full Ironman distance one day in training just to say I did it.*

BUILDING YOUR RACE PLAN

Everything you do during training has relevance to race day. The worksheets and checklists in your Ironplanner will guide you to keep track of the most important information. Keeping track of things along the way seems tedious at first with race day still far off, but it is easier than sitting down a week before your race trying to remember what you did.

IMAGINE BEING THERE

If you spend time imagining yourself at the race before it happens, you will feel calmer about it as race day nears. Hopefully you can get to a point where imagining yourself at the start line does not make you break into a sweat. That is a tall order.

Seeing yourself at the race does wonders for reducing anxiety, but it also allows you to practice overcoming hardship and makes the day go more smoothly. It prepares your nervous system for the challenge ahead. The more detailed your imagery, the more helpful it will be.

There are different perspectives you can use. You can see yourself through a camera's eye or see the event unfold through your own eyes, or switch between the two. Use whichever form is easiest for you, but take the time to go through the entire race day in your mind. The more you practice, the easier it gets.

Imagine race morning, the start, the swim and T1 for the duration of at least 3 long swims. Try to do some long swims at the same time of day that you will be racing. During your long rides, imagine coming out of T1 and getting through the entire course, into T2. Do at least one long ride at the time you will be riding on race day. See the course in your mind.

Repeat the process during some long runs. Do at least one in the afternoon, starting near the time you will be running. Figure out where you will be at sunset. In your mind, start with coming out of T2 and put yourself there all the way to the finish line.

As your preparation progresses, imagine yourself using the mental tools you have formulated. When you come up with new ideas, write them down in our training log or in the appropriate section of your Ironplanner.

Finally, imagine things going wrong and how you will overcome them. What if your goggles break or are lost? No problem, imagine yourself being OK with that and enjoying your swim anyway. Envision getting a flat tire and changing it without suffering an emotional meltdown. Anticipate stomach problems on the run, how will you handle them?

Don't forget to imagine the finish. Ponder it, dream it and believe that it will happen.

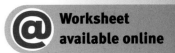
VISUALIZATION CHECKLIST

Use this checklist to help you imagine the race.

Imagine...
Waking up on race day and getting to the race venue
Setting up in the transition area
Getting your wetsuit on and getting into the water
Being in the water or on the beach with all the other athletes, waiting for the start
The National Anthem
The gun going off
The first half of the swim, being jostled around
The turnaround
The second half of the swim
Athletes passing you and you passing others
A variety of weather conditions
Nearing the swim finish
Exiting the water
Wetsuit removal
Getting ready in T1
Getting settled on the bike Bike
Aid stations on the bike – handing off bottles, etc.
First part of the ride (mile 1-37) What if you lose a bottle?
Athletes passing you and you passing others. You are unphased

Middle part of the ride (mile 38-75)
Will you want your special needs bag?
Last part of the ride (mile 76-112)
Things going wrong on the bike – flat/mechanical. You overcome
Seeing other athletes suffering, ill, withdrawing from the race
Getting ready for the run
Leaving T2
The first 2 miles of run
The first part of the run (mile 1-9) and aid stations, where are the hills?
The second part of the run (mile 9-18) and aid stations, special needs?
Seeing other athletes suffering, ill, withdrawing from the race. You go on with continued optimism
Will you want your special needs bag?
Bad patches during the run. Overcoming them
The last miles of the run, feeling remarkably good
Hearing the announcer in the distance at the finish line
Realizing that you are going to make it. Is it dark out?
The half mile, your speed picking up for the finish. Race officials guiding you to the finish line
Rounding the last corner, seeing the finish line, the crowd roaring, all pain is gone. The emotion wells-up and you cross the line **You are an Ironman!**

THE TAPER

Training takes a lot out of you physically and mentally. Your body needs some extra rest so that your cells can absorb the benefits of the training you have done. The reduced training load will do wonders for the as-yet-unseen injuries that are waiting to spring forth. Damaged cells will mend stronger than before so you will be in tip-top shape on race day.

Be careful with your body. Train less and don't stub your toe or trip over your sandals.

It is almost inevitable that you will find a way to bang yourself up before the race. Try not to. Even if you don't hurt yourself, expect to feel some phantom pain during this time. Don't worry, it will go away.

As your training volume decreases, you will find yourself with more time on your hands and renewed energy. It is tempting to get to some of the tasks you have been putting off, but don't do them. Wait until the race is over.

Your brain must rest as well. New projects require creative energy, which is one of your most powerful resources on race day.

Ideally, you will have a boring taper with some time to rehearse the mental strategies you have developed during training. Find activities that are calming and safe. Watch movies (at home, not in crowded theatres) and read.

5

MENTAL TOOLKIT 2: RACE DAY

A wandering mind can lead you to a bad place on race day. The key to everything is focus. The question is: what will you focus on?

Without pre-planned strategies, the mind tends to wander. You get tired and hardly notice when your brain starts playing games to get you to stop. You start having negative thoughts about your ability to perform, your performance suffers, then you get depressed about it and your performance suffers even more. This downward spiral of despair is enemy number one.

Focusing on something of your choosing will help you manage emotions, avoid negative thoughts and maintain form. Your thoughts are the key to staying relaxed, overcoming hardships, and doing the tasks necessary for a successful race day.

The mental strategy that you develop by completing the worksheets in this chapter will be put into your race plan. Some parts will be with you as notes on race day.

Mental training is often a limited endeavor among athletes who want to spend their time working-out. For Iron-distance racing, mental preparation it is a necessity. The more you do, the better, but it is time consuming. The strategies discussed herein originated from several books* and are distilled here into simple form. Focus and imagination are the weapons of mass destruction for the battles of will that face you during training and on race day. Learn to use them during training, so you can apply them on race day. Put the best ones in your race plan in Chapter 9.

ABOUT SWIMMING

Most triathletes train in swimming pools and workouts are dictated by distance (yardage, meters, laps). It is nearly impossible to count laps and use focusing strategies at the same time. Sometimes it is hard enough just to count laps. It is important to practice some mental techniques during your swim training so convert distance to time on occasion.

Since the swim is the first part of the race, it is most likely that the mental strategies you will need will be more about staying calm and fluid rather than distracting yourself from fatigue.

Ironman races are notorious for their mass starts. Depending on the race, you can count on a good amount of jostling during the swim. The most helpful things to remember are:
- Other swimmers are not kicking you on purpose so don't get mad. Save your energy for other things.
- Stay very loose, not rigid. If you get hit, pushed or kicked, just let your body give and bend into the blow.
- If you get short of breath, relax, and slow down. Your Ironman dream will not crumble because your swim is a bit slower than you hoped.
- All of those bodies create a draft. Whether you intend to take advantage of it or not, your swim time will probably be faster than you predict so relax.

SLICE IT UP

Breaking each part of the race into thin slices is a mental trick to help you focus. As you fatigue, your ability to concentrate weakens and it gets harder to focus on any one thing for very long. Slicing the race into small pieces shortens the amount of time that you need to maintain continuous focus.

Many races have done this for you with multiple loops for the bike and run portion. Calculate how long it will take to travel each loop or half-loop if you prefer. As the day gets longer, the slices should get smaller. The middle of the run is often the most difficult and by then you should have strategies for each mile. If you suffer a meltdown, your slices should be even thinner. Slices can be distances, or time periods, or a combination of both. The Race Slices Worksheet will give you some ideas for slicing up your race.

As you learn to manage your mental state with focus and imagination, decide where and when to apply the various strategies discussed in this chapter. If you are going to divide the ride into 18-mile slices in your mind on race day, do it in your training too. Ride for 18 miles then turn around, making your own loop. Through rehearsal you will grow accustomed to applying your mental strategies for the same time periods as the race. The rehearsal prepares your nervous system for the challenge ahead.

By race day you will have a practiced, specific plan for each slice of the race. Incorporate this into your race plan.

If you practice enough, the tools will become second nature. The ones you have not memorized can be written on small notes and carried with you on race day as discussed later in this chapter.

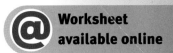

RACE SLICES WORKSHEET

- Is the swim start in the water or on the beach?

- Is the swim course out and back?

- Where are the buoys?

- How many loops are there on the bike course?

- How far is each loop?

- How long will it take to ride each way on each loop?

- Find a training route that is approximately the same distance as a single loop.

- If the bike course is out and back, where is the turn-around?

- If the bike course is point to point, where is the 37 mile mark? 75 miles?

- Where are the aid stations?

- Where are the landmarks?

- How many loops are there on the run?

- How far is each loop?

- How long will it take to run each loop?

- If the run is out and back, where it the turn around?

- If the run is point-to-point, where is the 10k, halfway, 30k, finish?

- Where are the aid stations?

- Where are the spectators?

- Where are the landmarks?

- If you plan to use a run-walk strategy, what will the time ratios be?

PROCESS GOALS

Process Goals are specific rules you make for yourself. The rules must address only things you have control over; your actions and thoughts. Process goals include racing intensity (heart rate or rate of perceived exertion), fueling schedules and mental strategies.

Because your speed and race time is subject to weather and other factors outside your control, it is not among your process goals. A time goal is something to have in the back of your mind as a motivation, but that magic number is only possible if you achieve your process goals.

The process goals are the meat of your race. You will come up with them during training when experience will show what works:

For the swim, process goals are usually technique reminders:
• Roll to the air
• Look down
• Stretch through the tunnel
• Smooth

For the bike, process goals are usually very precise because you get constant feedback from your cycling computer. Every computer shows speed, but that is of little help because it is subject to variables like wind and terrain. It says little about your exertion which is among the most crucial process goals. Controlling exertion is another word for pacing yourself. It is difficult to monitor how hard you are working when you are tired. You need a heart rate monitor or power meter for that. Cadence is particularly important for Ironman races, but not all cycling computers display it. Invest in one that does.

Here are examples of process goals for the bike leg:
• The heart rate you can maintain during a very long ride.

- The cadence and gearing that keeps you moving well for many hours.
- Reminders that help with your form.
- Preventative measures like stretching every 30 min.
- Drink enough so that you feel the urge to urinate 2 hours into the bike leg.
- Fueling details-how many swallows of Gatorade or how many gels at what time interval, every 15 minutes? Every 30? See Chapter 6 for fueling details.

Use your heart rate monitor on the run. Staying within the appropriate heart rate range, as dictated by your coach or training plan, will improve your chances of getting to the finish line with your stomach contents intact and a smile on your face. Here are some process goals for the run.

- The heart rate you can maintain for each slice (as you have defined it, above) of the race.
- If you are feeling good at the halfway point, you may allow yourself a higher heart rate range so you can pick up your speed.
- Form reminders like standing up straight, light feet and high elbows.
- Fueling details. Often the best laid fueling plans go awry on the run. At the very least, plan for how often to refuel, if not the calorie source (Gatorade, soup, solids, etc.)
- Keeping your feet dry to avoid blisters.

If you follow your process goals you will have a successful day. You can take it one step further and have different process goals for each slice of the race.

You will need 3-4 of these goals for each part of the race, and a few for the transitions too, like:

- Walk out of the water.
- Dry off before changing your shirt.
- Put on race belt with number.

ALARMS

If you use heart rate zones to monitor exertion level, use one with an alarm that will sound whenever you go outside the range you designate. This will help to keep your pace in check early in the bike leg, when it feels easy.

The alarm goes off whenever you go above your designated zone. You can also set an alarm to remind you to refuel. Missing even a single feeding can quickly lead to a bonk. Keeping track of feedings by time rather than distance provides a more steady flow of fuel than aid station to aid station.

If you use a run-walk strategy, a countdown alarm is crucial. In Ironman races and long workouts it is nearly impossible to keep your attention on your watch the entire time. If you plan a 9 min-1 min ratio, set the alarm to sound every 10 minutes. The first round will be a 10 minute run, then when the alarm sounds, walk for 60 seconds then run again until the alarm goes off. Sometimes counting steps is easier than glancing repeatedly at your watch waiting for a minute to pass, especially in the dark. If you plan to run in the dark, figure out how to turn the watch light on before race day so you aren't fumbling around pushing the wrong button during the race.

If you are going to put on a heart rate monitor, watch, or both in the transition area, be sure to program the alarms before race day and pack the wrist units in your bag such that the settings will not get fouled up when the bag is jostled around.

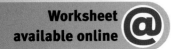
PROCESS GOALS WORKSHEET

Use this sheet to develop process goals. Try several and transfer the best ones to your Race Plan.

Process Goals	Swim	Transition 1
1		
2		
3		
4		

Process Goals	Bike part 1 ( )	Bike part 2 ( )	Bike part 3 ( )
1			
2			
3			
4			

PROCESS GOALS WORKSHEET SAMPLE

Use this sheet to develop process goals. Try several of them out. Transfer the best ones to your Race Plan later.

Process Goals	Swim	Transition 1
1	*Look down*	*No running*
2	*Heart rate low*	*Take the time*
3	*Roll to the air*	*Helmet on first*

These bike goals are identical for each section. You may wish to have different ones for each section.

Process Goals	Bike part 1 (loop 1)	Bike part 2 (loop 2)	Bike part 3 (loop3)
1	*No spikes in heart rate*	*No spikes in heart rate*	*No spikes in heart rate*
2	*Heart rate under 145*	*Heart rate under 145*	*Heart rate under 150*
3	*Fuel every 15 Min.*	*Fuel every 15 Min.*	*Fuel every 15 Min.*
4	*Cadence over 90 rpm*	*Cadence over 90 rpm*	*Cadence over 90 rpm*

Process Goals	Transition 2
1	
2	
3	
4	

Process Goals	Run part 1 ( )	Run part 2 ( )	Run part 3 ( )
1			
2			
3			
4			

PROCESS GOALS WORKSHEET SAMPLE

Process Goals	Transition 2
1	Take my time
2	Apply skin lubricant to hot spots
3	Take in some calories
4	Change shirt

Here, the run is divided into parts by miles and the goals are different for each part.

Process Goals	Run part 1 (Mile 1-9)	Run part 2 (Mile 10-19)	Run part 3 (Mile 20-Finish)
1	Heart rate under 140	Heart rate under 140	Heart rate under 150
2	2 gulps fuel every aid station	2 gulps fuel every aid station	2 gulps fuel every aid station
3	Keep feet dry	Keep feet dry	Run-walk 5:1 to mile 23, then no walking
4	Run-walk 9 min:1 min (9:1)	Run-walk 9:1 to mile 13, then 5:1	Smile and run through the finish

SHIFTING FOCUS

Controlling your thoughts is the key to emotional control. Emotional control will get you through an Ironman. Practice focusing during training and it will be easier on race day.

FOCUSING OUT

There are times when focusing on the external world will serve you well. It is most helpful early in the race or training session, when you feel good and your form hasn't fallen apart. By focusing outward for the first hour, you can collect some memories and the time will go more quickly.

It is simple; just keep a lookout for something you can tell your kid about (or your spouse or your dog) when you get home. Maybe you saw a bird that was an astounding shade of blue. Maybe you saw a kid on a Batman bike and it jolted you into the thundering soundtrack from the movie, making you smile. These are small things, but when training is over you will remember the blue bird and the Batman bike, not how many hours you rode or how much it hurt.

Focusing outward is also helpful late in the race when you need a short (up to 30 min.) mental vacation from all the pedaling and running.

Outward focus has its limitations; when you focus outward, you are not paying attention to your form or your process goals and thoughts tend to drift through your brain at random. If you focused outward the entire race, you would get bored and your thoughts would start drawing you emotionally downward in an effort to make you stop.

FOCUSING IN

Focusing in means concentrating on the thoughts that will be most helpful in your quest, either to the end of the training session or to the finish line on race day. Which thoughts should you focus on? That is what this chapter will show you. As you complete the worksheets, you will create specific strategies that you can test in training. Those that are particularly helpful will be put into your race plan in Chapter 9.

If you don't control your focus, your thoughts will eventually hinder your race performance. The more often you practice focusing in, the easier it becomes.

During your race you will seek a steady emotional state. At times you will feel very tired and it will take a lot of effort to hold your focus and stay steady. The more tired you are, the more your brain will rely on simple, repeated messages.

Process goals will always be among those messages. By the time you race you will have 3-4 process goals that you automatically use for each event.

Other thoughts will come from the worksheets in this chapter. If your emotions or your body start to crumble, you will have to direct your attention to the cause of your distress. Often, if your emotional state takes a dive, it is a signal to eat. Information on managing a meltdown appears later in this chapter.

After many hours of concentration, shifting focus outward again for a few minutes will provide a refreshing mental break. Aid stations are a good time to do this. Don't linger too long in your mental vacation though; sliding into the pit of despair can happen quickly if you are not paying attention.

BEST MOMENTS

When things are going badly, it is difficult to change your emotional state. The struggles you will face on race day can drag you down mentally and physically. You can escape by focusing on happy, empowering memories, but which ones?

Without practice, it is difficult to come up with these memories on race day. Don't worry, you can come up with them now and list them on your Best Moments Worksheet. This will bring them back to life. When you hit a bad patch during the race, you can open the spigot and let them spill out over you.

Don't limit yourself to memories of athletic success. Brainstorm. Your goal is to list memories of *any kind* that had strong emotional impact; the ones that made you feel powerful, competent and valuable.

Your Ironman training will provide many joyful moments and opportunities to overcome adversity. Rigorous training seems to heighten the emotions, so seemingly trivial events can become lasting memories, especially if you are looking for them. Look for them and add them to your list. Bathe in them often.

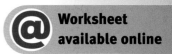
BEST MOMENTS WORKSHEET (EXAMPLE)

The birth of my daughter, that first moment of looking upon her. Reaching my weight loss goal and keeping it off for 5 years. The feeling of approaching the finish of my first marathon...

SEEK INSPIRATION

You already have a healthy dose of inspiration if you have entered an Ironman-distance race but you will need an ongoing supply to get through what lies ahead.

Seek inspiration in books, magazines and DVD's. Watch Ironman videos on YouTube.com. Clip inspiring photos from magazines and put them in view. Find inspiration in others that are overcoming hardship to live better. Imagine your favorite athletes in their suffering and moments of glory.

Include people that have inspired you and dedicate miles or portions of the race to them. Tell them you want to dedicate a particular mile to them. They will be pleased. On race day, imagine them being with you. Have an imaginary conversation with them. It can be a lifeboat when you need it most, out there alone on the race course.

Be a sponge to inspiration. Use it to transform your emotional state. Use the Inspiration worksheet to write cues that trigger memories that inspire you. Use the cues during training and include the best ones in your Race Plan.

North American Sports has made the "Ironman" a product but I don't mind. It has given me the vision of a dream that is true and real and personal. It is not fake.

A triathlete suffering on the Queen K is the ultimate vision of athleticism and raw sex appeal. The annual telecast of the World Championship is like an IV, feeding my blood with inspiration.

INSPIRATION WORKSHEET (EXAMPLE)

The film of Rick and Dick Hoyt charging across the Ironman finish line. Imagining how hard it was for my sister to drive to the hospital for cancer surgery. The photos of Ironman legends up on my wall. How much they suffered for those victories...

ʒUS ON MANTRAS

A mantra is a single word or phrase that triggers a desired response in you. Repeating a powerful mantra during the race can help you dig deeper, calm you down, or just keep you moving. The world is full of mantras, but you can also make up your own. The only ones that matter are the ones that *speak to you*. Write them on your Mantra List and use them when you need a boost during training. Include the good ones in your Race Plan.

Here are some examples:

- Transcend
- No Problem
- Keep on keeping on
- Pain is temporary, pride is forever
- Nice and easy
- I won't back down
- Relax and slide
- Glide, Calm, Ignore
- Steady and smooth
- Push it now
- Plenty of Air
- Use the juice
- Dance over the path
- As the day gets longer, I get stronger

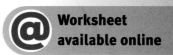
MANTRA WORKSHEET (EXAMPLE)

I move forward in bliss. Thank you for this day, for this moment to live. Just keep swimming, swimming, swimming...

HAVE A THEME

Put together a sentence to describe your approach to each portion of
the race. For instance, "the swim will be a bath, the bike leg will be a
ride on the wind and the run will be a day in the park." The theme
sets the tone for the event. It should make the day sound like a series
of achievable and enjoyable tasks. Put it into your race plan. When you
get anxious, just remember your theme and feel better.

RACE DAY THEME WORKSHEET (EXAMPLE)

The swim is so full of flow. The current pushes me effortlessly along. The bike is a vacation from the scrambling of everyday life. All I hear is the hum of tires. The run will take me into the sunset and lead me to the full moon...

IMAGINE THE BATTLE

Make a mental picture of troublesome thoughts and feelings that plague you during endurance events. It may be anxiety, despair, fear or something else. Drawing a picture of the bad feeling is the first step to mastering it. Once you have drawn the villain, give it a name. The more ridiculous the image, the easier it will be to remember.

When things get difficult in a race, positive thoughts and feelings go to war with the villain you have identified. Imagine how the good guys will win. This is up to you to figure out.

...The negative thoughts that come when I am fatigued are "Goblutes." I see them as little grey amoeba-like splotches. They are ugly and they multiply quickly. The more Goblutes there are, the worse I feel.

Goblutes can be defeated in 2 ways. They can be obliterated by high-powered automatic machine guns, which spatter them to bits in an instant. The machine guns work well when the Goblutes are just starting to appear and there are not too many of them. When the number of Goblutes gets out of hand, I call in the heavy-stuff, the dogs.

Everyone knows that dogs will eat anything and they love Goblutes. I imagine ugly mutts lapping up the Goblutes, tails wagging. Each dog is a memory of something I did or experienced that was good, happy, empowering, funny, or impressive. When the Goblutes threaten, I imagine them being eaten by the dogs and I feel better.

Use your Race Resume, Best Moments, Inspirations and Mantras as ammunition for defeating the villain that haunts you. Take your time and create something meaningful.

You knew this was coming... Here is a space for you to sketch your heroes and villains. Think if it as a story board which you will refine over time.

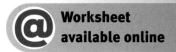

BATTLE WORKSHEET (EXAMPLE)

Imagine what fatigue looks like and make a sketch of it. How will you defeat the fatigue monster? This sketch will come to you when you need it and it will probably make you laugh, but it will help you feel stronger too...

More and more green blobs of goo appear as I get tired. I send a bomb filled with good memories and ...

MAKE MAGIC

Magic is most helpful when you need a strong boost. It only works for short periods of time. Create an image of something magical that you can infuse into your legs to give them a new source of strength. When you need some extra "oomph," draw some of the magic into your legs. Feel your legs filling with energy.

This works particularly well during high intensity training, when your muscles are starting to burn. It is also useful when you notice that you are slowing down.

Example: Imagine a treasure chest filled with liquid gold. You can ladle the gold like honey into your muscles. The gold is full of oxygen and magical properties that will give you extra power, endurance and feelings of success. There is an endless supply of gold.

Create your own image of magic strength and put it into your notebook.

MAGIC WORKSHEET (EXAMPLE)

If you could pour pure energy into your tired legs, what would it look like? Imagine magic stuff that takes all the pain away and gives you effortless velocity...

PUT IT ALL TOGETHER

Congratulate yourself for working through every checklist and worksheet in this section. Your toolkit is full. Next you will put the most helpful tools into your race plan. Below is an illustration of how the tools can be combined into a mental strategy for the run portion of the race.

SAMPLE MENTAL STRATEGY FOR RUN:

Mile 1-8

Finding my groove, easy and smooth. ← Theme/mantra
Focus Out, see landmarks and Best Moments

- HR under 150
- Run : Walk 9:1, ← Process Goals
- 2 gulps fuel/aid station
- Dry Feet

Mile 9-16

Focus, Imagination & Inspiration

Cruising on a Sunday Afternoon
Focus in, gliding up the final hill full of momentum. (Imagine *The Battle* as needed.)
McCormack on Queen K.
Celebrate mile 13 with Best Moments in training.
Fill my legs with liquid gold – there is plenty left.
Focus out at mile 15. Count tattoos, greet other athletes.

- HR under 150
- Run : walk 5:1
- 2 gulps fuel/aid station

- Dry Feet
- Huge smile for all spectators

Mile 17-Finish   ← Race Slice

Fly Downhill   Mile Dedications
Focus (written on bracelet):

| Mile 18: Coach | Mile 20: USMC | Mile 23: Dad |
| Mile 19: Mom | Mile 22: Mark | Mile 24: *Fly Now* |

- HR under 158
- Run:walk 5:1 to mile 20, then 9:1 or none
- 2 gulps fuel/aid station
- Stand up tall

MAKE NOTES TO HELP YOU REMEMBER

On race day it will be difficult to remember more than a few process goals, especially late in the race when you will need your mental tools the most. You can carry a small list with you for the bike leg, and another for the run. Print the list in a small but readable font, in a shape and size that you can mount on your bike or put on your wrist. Both should be covered with clear postal tape to keep the moisture out. Attach the list to your bike on race day and put the bracelet in your bike to run bag so you can slip it on at T2.

SAMPLE RACE BRACELET

- Content is up to you. Consider text, drawings, color.
- Use a font style and size you can read while you are moving.
- Cut it out and seal it with clear postal tape for waterproofing and durability.
- If you need a lot of space, make it reversible and write on both sides.
- Keep it after the race. Battered and worn, it is a great memento.

Mantras

Mile Dedications

Memory forever * No Problem * Overcome * Stand Up * Fly * Won't Back Down

16-Mom 17-Dad 18-Bob 19-Jill 20-Coach 21-USMC 22-Barry 23-Kids 24-Flying 25-look alive

70.3 run * Hill St. * A Wonderful Night * Race at Lake * Award * Steel legs * Coffee blues

Best Moments

MANAGING A MELTDOWN

A meltdown occurs when you experience physical discomfort so extreme that you are not sure you will be able to finish the race. There are many possible causes, but often the root cause has to do with fueling, hydration, heat, or a combination. The first step in overcoming it is to evaluate what is happening.

If the main problem is your emotional state, take in some calories and you might feel better quickly. You may also feel a little dizzy if you are bonking. Again, take in some fuel and see if your symptoms resolve in a few minutes. If your symptoms are severe get medical help immediately.

Slowing down will slow your heart rate and allow digestion to proceed more easily. It will also allow you to cool off.

You may have to stop, but that is not the end of the world. Even if you vomit, you will feel better shortly. Many athletes stop, get sick, recover, and then continue on the finish the race. Decide that you *will* finish, no matter what and be prepared with your mental tools.

- Focus on smaller slices. Look for landmarks that are close by and get to those. Repeat for as long as it takes to finish.
- Focus outward for a little while. Talk to someone a little.
- Imagine The Battle you created a few pages ago.
- Remember your Best Moments in training and in life.
- Think about people that inspire you. Remember Ironman athletes like Jon Blais, and Dick and Rick Hoyt, who became Ironmen in the face of much greater hardships than what you are experiencing.
- Think about the people that are waiting for you to finish.
- Use your best mantras.
- Remember the finish you imagined during training. Know that it can still happen. Bask in how glorious it will feel to run across that line.
- Finish. Whatever you do, just get there. No matter what the outcome, you will remember it for the rest of your life.

* *Going Long: Training for Iron-Distance Triathlons,* Joe Friel and Gordon Byrn
Mental Training for Triathlons, Jim Taylor, Ph.D and Terri Schneider
The Lore of Running, Tim Noakes, M.D., Fourth Edition
The New Toughness Training For Sports, James E. Loehr

6

FUELING

Fueling is about providing your body with what it needs to get through the race. Nutrition is everything else having to do with food. By race day, you must know how many calories per hour you can comfortably metabolize, in what form those calories will take, and how often you should ingest them. Working through this chapter will help you devise a tested fueling plan that you can have confidence in.

The trick in long-distance races is to fuel for the duration while minimizing the risk of gastrointestinal (GI) upset. Much has been written on the subject but ultimately you will have to develop a plan that works for you. Use the 3 worksheets in this chapter to eliminate culprits and find the right type and amount of fuel for you to use on race day.

ELIMINATE CULPRITS

Start with eliminating fuels that give you gas, bloating or feel like they are sitting in your stomach. Minor discomfort is enough. The discomfort can magnify over the course of a long session as you consume more and more. To assure that the distress is from the type of fuel rather than the amount, consume no more than 8 oz every 15 minutes. Don't guzzle too much fluid at one time.

Consider your pre-workout meal. If high protein sits in your stomach, note it in Fuel Worksheet #1. If pancakes are perfect, note that down in worksheet #2 as a fuel that seems fine.

Keep the labels of fuels that cause problems during training sessions and eventually you will find primary ingredients common to all of the ones that give you trouble. Often it is the form of sugar that is the culprit (like anything ending in "-ose"). Many fuels have artificial sweeteners that cause problems. Fuels that contain fat sometimes sit in your stomach. Salt tablets can sit there as well. Record the information in Fueling worksheet #1.

Experiment during long training sessions at race intensity, especially long runs following several hours on the bike. It is during the run that the problems are most likely to occur. Record the information in Fueling worksheet #1.

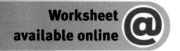
WORKSHEET #1—Fuels that bother you.

Record information from fuels that cause even minor distress: gas, bloating, sitting in your stomach. Listed are common ingredients in race fuels. Put a checkmark next to the ones contained in problem fuels.

Ingredients	Fuel name:	Fuel name:	Fuel name:	Fuel name:	Fuel name:
Caffeine					
Calcium					
Citric acid					
Dextrose					
Fat					
Fiber					
High fructose corn syrup					
Glucose					
Magnesium					
Maltodextrin/ glucose polymers					
Potassium phosphate					
Potassium sorbate					
Protein/Amino acids					
Ribose					
Sodium					
Soy protein					
Sucrose					
Other					

GASTROINTESTINAL ISSUES

GI issues can be as mild as gas and as horrific as vomiting and bloody diarrhea. Not only is it uncomfortable, but moderate to severe symptoms indicate calories are sitting in your stomach, not being absorbed. So not only do you feel poorly, but your body can't get the fuel it needs. GI problems are a double-whammy and are very common in the Iron-distance events.

Some athletes suffer with GI issues on every run. If you are one of these unlucky souls, don't despair. There are things you can do to manage the problem. The internet is full of helpful articles, especially directed toward runners. Here are some suggestions:

- What you eat the day before a long/hard run will influence what occurs during the run the next morning. Stay away from high fiber and "high yield" foods. Dairy can cause problems as well.

- Over-the-counter medications such as Imodium and Pepto Bismol can help when taken before your workout. These products work differently so if one fails, try the other. It may take an hour or more for the benefit to really kick in, so as always, experiment. Short, intense races are a good testing ground.

- Carry your medication of choice with you on race day. Bring a few moist "baby wipes" with you in a small Ziploc bag in your pocket.

- A belly-full of liquid carbohydrate just asks for trouble. Some potions cause more GI issues than others, another reason to experiment with different types.

- Dehydration can contribute to GI problems, but so can gulping more liquid than you can process. Drink enough fluid, in the form of potion and water, so that you have the urge to urinate 2 hours into the bike leg.

- Wear black shorts on race day.

- GI distress can be overcome even during the race. Usually it is a matter of laying off the carbohydrate drinks, slowing down to allow the gut to absorb the calories and liquid that are already there, and focusing on water until you feel better. Even if you have to stop and sit, the race is not lost. Prepare for this possibility and vow to handle it with patience.

Gastrointestinal troubles are caused by ingesting the wrong amount of the wrong fuel for a given race intensity. Worksheet #1 will help you identify ingredients to avoid.

THE SWIM

The swim does not offer many opportunities for fueling. A quick sip of carbohydrate drink or an energy gel right before the start can be helpful, but not if you are prone to seasickness. The bike leg is the main attraction as far as fueling goes.

THE BIKE

You need to keep yourself going and also set yourself up for the run later. Find out what will be served on the race course. If Gatorade is your drink of choice and they will serve it at the race, you need not carry your own. If you need a different potion to avoid GI problems, you will have to carry it with you. You might also decide to use a combination of race-provided fuels and your own.

Once you have decided what fuel works best, you have to get it on your bike. One of the best ways to carry liquid fuel is with a single, highly concentrated bottle, used in combination with water which is provided on the course.

Carbo-Pro is particularly easy to make in high concentrat
available in powder and also in a liquid, called Carbo-Pro
liquid form has some additional ingredients, including el
and comes in 1200 calorie bottles. They are handy for pu
your special needs bag. Adding a few 100-calorie scoops of Carbo-Pro
powder into a ready made Carbo-Pro 1200 bottle is a quick and easy
way to pack a lot of calories into a small space.

Don't forget electrolytes. Some liquid fuels have them, most do not.
They are available in tablets and capsules. If the tablets don't sit well,
try emptying a few capsules into your drink bottle.

Caffeine can also be used effectively. It is remarkable how much better
one can feel with a little caffeine, especially coffee addicts that have
been deprived of their multi-cup fix on race day. Power Gel now comes
with both electrolytes and caffeine. Figure out what works for you.

Here are instructions for making a concentrated fuel potion for a 6
hour ride:

1. Estimate your calorie requirements at 200 calories per hour for a
   small woman, up to 500 calories an hour for a large man. The
   average is about 300 calories.

2. Do the math: 6 hours x 300 cal/hr=1800 calories.

3. Using a typical powdered fuel, you will need 18 x 100-calorie
   scoops. Put the powder in the bottle first.

4. Fill the bottle with water and mix the powder in.

5. Draw lines around the bottle with a permanent marker so that the
   bottle is divided into 6 equal portions.

6. Each portion is enough calories for one hour. Drink fresh water with
   the fuel and take several small feedings per hour.

7. If the fluid is too syrupy you will have to put less powder into the bottle and more water. That means there will be fewer calories. You can make up the calorie deficit with gel. A 1200 calorie bottle, plus 6 (100 cal ea.) is 1800 calories. Adjust as needed.

The longer you will be on your bike, the more fuel you will need. Extra large bottles will carry 32 oz. But they are hard to find. Look on the internet. If you find one, make sure it will fit on your frame.

If you are going to use gels or bars, figure out how you will open them mid-ride. Taping gels to the top tube works well because as you remove the packet, you tear the top off. You can eat the gel without ever touching the sticky end of the package You can fill your jersey pockets with snacks and put a carrier (Bento) box on your top tube. There is a limit to the number of gels and bars you can carry. Alternating solids and liquids is not only more palatable, but it makes it easier to pack sufficient fuel on your bike using the various methods discussed here. Test your fuels before race day.

You will also have to figure out how to dispose of empty wrappers. Littering is a rule violation subject to penalty. If you drop a wrapper or bottle, you are expected to stop and pick it up. Jersey pockets work well, but many triathlon tops have inadequate pockets. Tucking empty wrappers into the leg of your shorts is handy, but the residue eventually ends up on your legs. Make sure the package is really empty before doing this.

STICKINESS

Sticky fingers may be as much the mark of an amateur cyclist as grease is on your calves, but for some it is inevitable. Here are some suggestions:

- If using a Profile Design bottle between your aero bars, fill it with water only so when you get splashed, it is with clear water and not sticky energy drink.

- If you use a Profile Design Bottle between your aero bars, tape a small plastic bag between your aero bars, behind the bottle. Tuck empty wrappers down into the bag, like putting pennies in a piggy bank. The bag will be hidden from the wind.

- Wear full-finger cycling gloves. When your fingers get sticky, you won't feel it.

If you decide to rely upon aid stations for calories on race day, you should still carry some calories with you. If you have a mechanical problem on the bike, you may have to walk your bike to the next aid station for help. If you do not have fuel, you will deprive your body of calories during that time.

Experiment with breakfasts too. Try alternatives that are easy to make and easy to pack. Being able to bring your own breakfast food for race morning is one less thing to worry about.

THE RUN

The closest you can get to a race simulation is a long bike ride followed by a long run. The fuel that serves you well on the bike may lose its appeal after 112 miles. You may not be able to swallow gels at all. Solids might be completely repulsive.

During long bricks, use your chosen bike potion then switch to the race fuel on your run. If it feels OK, you know that is an option. If it sends you running for the bathroom, you will have to find an alternative.

Carry fuel as liquid or as powder that you mix with water at aid stations. Various hydration configurations are available to try: fuel belts, camelbacks and hand-held bottles. Test them out for comfort before the race. Do the math and calculate how much you will have to carry. The body often tolerates a combination of fuels better than any single type. Combine your chosen fuel with the race day fare and you won't have to carry so much.

Even if you decide to use the products offered at the race, it is wise to have some emergency calories with you. If things get rough, having to get to the next aid station can take a long time.

KEEP TRACK

Read labels, measure and record accurate information. At times it will seem like a chemistry experiment because it is. The Fueling Worksheets only cover long sessions because those are the most relevant to race day.

FUELING WORKSHEETS

WORKSHEET #2—Foods that agree with you before long training sessions

Think in terms of breakfast on race day. Try foods that are easy to bring and that you can reheat in the microwave. If you have GI issues, stay away from dairy and high fiber foods.

Date	Workout	Fuel name and amount	Calories	Time between meal and swim	Repeat or avoid	Comments

WORKSHEET #3 — Fueling during 4+ hour workouts

Pay particular attention to fueling during long brick workouts (ride followed by run). A long ride followed by a run is the scenario most likely to cause problems. Take calories on the run even if you don't need them, to see what you can tolerate.

Date	Workout	Fuel name and amount	Calories: total and per hour	Fueling schedule	Repeat or avoid	Comments

7

TRAVEL & SPECTATORS

Races fill early as do the most convenient hotels. Make your reservations early and reconfirm several times before race day.

TIMING

You have to arrive in time to check-in for the race. Many races require check-in 2 days before the event. Confirm this before you make any plans. Record the check-in time on the Travel Worksheet in this chapter. If you are traveling by air, give yourself ample time for flight delays and baggage foul-ups.

HOW LONG TO STAY

After the race you may be able to leave your bike and unclaimed gear bags securely overnight for pick-up the following day. The awards ceremony is the day after the race and this is also when the "finisher" merchandise is available at the race expo area. It is your best opportunity to socialize with the other athletes in a relaxed atmosphere. If you have a choice, plan to spend at least some of the post-race day participating in these activities. You will be glad you did.

LOCATION

Try to book a hotel that is very close to either the race venue or some portion of the race course. You will have to get to the race venue several times before race day (check-in, athlete meeting, swim practice, bike and race bag drop-off). Parking is usually at a premium and you don't want to tire your legs out with too much walking. You will need a course map. If the map for this year's race is not available, look at the one for last year. It is likely the route will be the same. A 1200 calorie bottle plus 6 (100 cal ea.) is 1800 total calories. Adjust as needed.

Make sure your hotel is close to a restaurant or offers a breakfast buffet at the very least. Your goal is to move around as little as possible before the race. It is tedious and time consuming to have to find a restaurant for every meal. The one you choose will probably be packed with other athletes and spectators. Along the same lines, check and see if your hotel has a refrigerator/microwave in the room so you can bring some of your own food.

Record the name, address and phone number of the hotel in both the Travel Worksheet and the Contacts and Facilities Appendix of your Ironplanner.

HOW MANY ROOMS?

Reserve an extra room or two for family and friends that later decide to join you. Make sure you can cancel your reservation a few days in advance of the race if need be.

SHIP YOUR BIKE

Once you have your hotel/accommodations in order, it is time to figure out how to get your bike there. There are several ways to do this. You can hire a company that will put your bike in a truck and drive it to the race, along with many other bikes. The advantage of this is that you do not have to disassemble and reassemble your bike at the race venue.

You can also bring your bike on your flight as baggage. It will have to be disassembled to some degree and packed in a box that the airline will accept.

The third option is to have the bike shipped separately via a commercial delivery service like UPS or FEDEX. Again, the bike will have to be disassembled and packed. Most bike shops will disassemble and pack your bike for you. This is worth the expense.

You can have your bike shipped to a local bike shop or to your hotel. The bike shop option has the advantage that a mechanic can reassemble the bike and check it over. Be sure to make arrangements for this beforehand so your bike will arrive in time for the shop to make the bike ready for you.

Make arrangements to ship your bike home after the race as well. Record this information in both the Travel section and the Contacts and Facilities Appendix of your Ironplanner.

TRAVEL WORKSHEET

Travel	Date	Amount paid/Due
Hotel name, address, phone #		
Confirmation # # of rooms		
Bike transport to race, assembly and check over details.		
Bike transport/packing home details.		
Travel to race city. Arrival + departure details		

Check in + out time	Confirm before race day	Cancel deadline

SPECTATORS

MAKE A SPECTATOR PACKET

The special people in your life will be heavily invested in your race so make it easy for them to share your triumphant day. Even if they can not be at the race venue, you can prepare a packet for them with all the vital information they will need:

- Spectator Meeting Places Worksheet from this chapter
- Course maps
- Ironmanlive.com information
- Your bib number
- Your Race Plan from chapter 9

Spectators will have a very long day waiting for you at the race venue. The better your plan, the more comfortable they will be. Most races will print information about road closures, parking and viewing suggestions. Check the race website a day or so before the race, print it out and put it in their Spectator packet.

Your hotel may have a race day shuttle and special breakfast accommodations for athletes and spectators. Take the time to plan a comfortable spot for your spectators to wait. Better still, use your Race Time Prediction Worksheet from Chapter 9 to designate

different meeting places at various times. This will give them freedom to roam, eat and participate in the festivities while you are out there living your dream.

SPECTATOR MEETING PLACES

Use the Race Time Prediction Worksheet from Chapter 9 to coordinate meeting places with your spectators.

Thanks to the internet, many Ironman races offer online athlete tracking. Log onto *www.ironmanlive.com* for real-time updates of athletes on the course. But beware, no race is perfect and even technology fails at times. The split times may not show in real-time. Certain splits may not show up at all if there is a technical problem. Spectators should simultaneously watch for your finish on the live video feed in case you finish before the internet information is updated.

GEAR PICK-UP

With proper ID, someone can retrieve your bike and gear bags from the transition area while you are running on race day. This is a lifesaver. The last thing you want to do after the race is walk anywhere unnecessarily and haul your bike and bags back to the car.

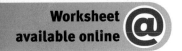

SPECTATOR MEETING PLACES WORKSHEET

Use information from your Time Prediction worksheet in Chapter 9.

Where I will be	When I expect to be at... Provide a time range with some margin for error/ unexpected problems	...where Possible meeting places
Race area		
Swim start		
Swim finish		
T1		
End of Bike loop 1/Mile #_____		
End of Bike loop 2/Mile #_____		
Bike finish		
T2		
End of Run loop 1/Mile #_____		
End of Run loop 2/Mile #_____		
Finish		

SPECTATOR MEETING PLACES WORKSHEET SAMPLE

Where I will be	When I expect to be... Provide a time range with some margin for error/ unexpected problems	...where Possible meeting places
Race area	6:00	At timing mat for swim start
Swim start	7:00	
Swim finish	8:15-8:25	Near transition tent
T1	8:28-8:38	
End of Bike loop 1/ Mile #_____	10:38-11:10	Stadium parking lot
End of Bike loop 2/ Mile #_____	12:55-1:40	Food Court
Bike finish	3:35-4:10	
T2	3:53-4:18	Aid station #1
End of Run loop 1/ Mile #_____	5:00-6:00	Same aid station
End of Run loop 2/Mile #_____	6:38-8:00	Same aid station
Finish	8:22-10:00	Near finish tape

RACE DAY BAGS

You will be given several bags to use on race day. It will be stressful to make decisions about these bags on the eve of the race so plan ahead. Read the race instructions to learn about when you have to drop the bags at the race venue and when you will have access to them. Pack each of these bags at home in garbage bags and label them clearly. Transfer the contents into the official race bags when you get there.

Each bag is listed, along with suggested contents. There is extra space for you to add other items. If you add to the lists as you think of things, your list should be complete by the time you have to pack the bags. There is a lost and found and items can be claimed the day after the race so mark your gear. Each bag is explained below.

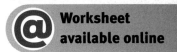

BAG #1 PRE-RACE DRY CLOTHES BAG

This is the bag you will bring with you on race morning. It should have the clothes you wear to the race venue, and other items you want to have before the race. You will probably have to bring your swim gear on race morning. Check the race instructions. You will get this bag back.

Pre-race snacks
Wetsuit
Anti-chaffing lotion
Swim cap
Timing chip if not already on your ankle
2 pairs of goggles

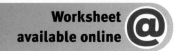
BAG #2 SWIM TO BIKE BAG:

This is the bag you will get in transition from the swim to the bike. When you get this bag back after the race, it will have your swim gear and everything you removed at T1. Volunteers may dump the contents onto the ground at your feet. To avoid damage, pack your sunglasses lightly in a box or case. Your race number will not last the day unless you reinforce it with postal/electrical tape where it attaches to your shirt/belt. You may be given an extra number to put into your bike to run bag, in case the original number falls off.

Bike Clothes
Bike Shoes
Socks
Helmet
Sunglasses
Gloves-consider full-finger if you dislike sticky fingers from gels and fluids
Lip Balm
Towel – compact chamois type
Anti-chaffing lotion
Race number attached to race belt and reinforced with tape

BAG # 3 SPECIAL NEEDS BIKE BAG (THROW-AWAY):

Think of the special needs bag as a lifeboat. If you have a mechanical or physical need during the race, getting to this bag will probably be quicker than waiting for help on the course, even if you have to push your bike for awhile to get to it.

Extra bottle of your nutrition drink in case you lose a bottle on the course
Snack that will make you happy
Minor medical-band aids, lip balm, anti-chaffing lotion
Spare tubes and air
Cycling Gloves
Dry socks

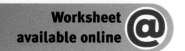
BAG #4 BIKE TO RUN BAG:

You will get this bag in transition from the bike to the run. It will contain everything you took off in T2. You will get this bag back after the race.

Run shoes
Dry socks
Run clothes
Hat
Sunglasses
Whatever you plan to carry with you on the run
Gel or other snack to eat while in transition
Extra race number

BAG #5 SPECIAL NEEDS RUN BAG (THROW AWAY):

This bag will be made available near the half-way point of the run. You are not required to use this bag during the race. Pack it as a throw away because you may not get it back after the race.

Minor medical – Vaseline, Pepto Bismol tablets, pain relievers, Band Aids
Dry socks
Clothing-long sleeved shirt if it gets cold
Fuel – special food that makes you happy

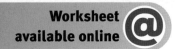
BAG #6 HOMEMADE FINISH LINE BAG

You may have to walk awhile to get to food after the race. Have someone meet you at the finish line with this bag and you can begin refueling right away.

Non-perishable food and drink
Warm clothes
Dry Socks

9

RACE PLAN

TIME PREDICTION

After the months of training and preparation, it can be intimidating to put pencil to paper and make your predictions. A Time Prediction Worksheet is provided in this chapter. It has space for your expected finish time and your dream time. Training pace during your long sessions is a good indicator of race pace. Allow for some slowing due to fatigue and unknown difficulties. Make it fun. Have your coach fill one out and compare them after the race.

Once you have filled it out, forget it. The only things you can control on race day are your behavior and your thoughts, which you have addressed in your process goals. Your speed will take care of itself.

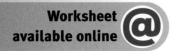
TIME PREDICTION WORKSHEET

	Dream Time		
	Time	**Clock (elapsed) time**	**Time of day**
Race Start Time:	Dream duration or split	Time displayed on official clock	Time of day (duration + start time)
Total Swim Time			
T1			
Total Bike Time			
T2			
Total Run Time			
Total Race Time			

Expected Time			Actual
Time	Clock (elapsed) time	Time of day	Time
Most likely duration or split	Time displayed on official clock at end	Time of day (duration + start time)	Actual duration or split

TIME PREDICTION WORKSHEET SAMPLE OF DREAM TIME CALCULATIONS

Preparing this worksheet is time consuming, but very helpful. Check your math a few times to make sure you have it right.

Dream Time

Time	Clock (elapsed)	Time of day
am duration or split time	Time on official clock	Time of day (duration + start time)
Start Time:		
7:00		
Total Swim Time — 1:20		
T1 — 0:08	1:28	8:28
Bike loop 1 — 2:15	3:43	10:43
loop 2 — 2:15	5:58	
loop 3 — 2:15	8:13	
Total Bike Time — 6:45	8:13	3:43
T2 — 00:10	8:23	3:53
Run loop 1 — 1:35	9:58	4:58
loop 2 — 1:40	11:38	6:38
loop 3 — 1:44	13:22	8:22
Total Run Time — 4:59	13:	
Total Race Time	13:	

Step 1: Enter time of day that the race will start.

Step 2: Put time estimates in this first column.

Step 3: Add all of the splits to determine the total amount of time you will be racing.

Step 4: Add the starting time of day (here 7) to amount of time you will be racing to determine time of day.

In this example, 7:00 + 13:22=20:22 hours. Convert this to time of day by subtracting 12:00.

A PERFECTLY PLANNED RACE

Writing your race plan is one of the last things you will do before race day, but it is the most important. Every list, schedule and worksheet you have used has created information to use in your Race Plan. It is the culmination of everything you know about getting through this event. It is your personal recipe for success.

Once the race plan is complete, use it as a cross-check to assure you have everything you will need in your race day bags. Double check your fueling needs and make sure you bring enough potion and bottles.

ASSEMBLING YOUR RACE PLAN

It is nice to have your entire race plan on a single sheet of paper. Due to size and margin considerations, it will be difficult to get all of the information on the Race Plan Worksheet in this book. Using the Race Plan Worksheet format, print your race plan on a standard 8 1/2 x 11 sheet of paper and divide it into 3 equal parts as in Fig. 2 below. Use one column for each discipline. Fold the sheet vertically so you can study one discipline at a time. Glance at it often in the week before the race to help you memorize it. Write the more detailed strategies for late in the run on a race bracelet to carry with you on the run. Use the format in the sample or create your own

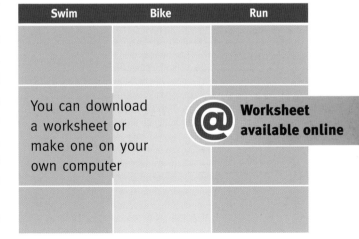

Fig 2. *Sample Race Plan*

RACE PLAN WORKSHEET-SAMPLE

Swim	Bike	Run
Out and back. Sun in eyes. Buoys on left.	2 loops, 4 parts. Hill at turnaround. Shopping Mall near end.	3 loops x 8.5 miles.
Family near wetsuit strippers-lake side.	Family at Mile 10, Mile 66.	Family at Mile markers 2, 11, 17, finish.
1:05-1:10	6.5-7 hours 1:40/part	5-5.5 hours (1:50/loop)
SWIM PLAN • Gel before start. • Keep heart low and slow. Calmly slipping through the hole.	PART 1 PLAN • Heart rate below 140. • No spikes. • cadence 90+. • Standard fueling Focus out. Glide. Calm. Ignore.	MILE 1-8 PLAN • HR under 150. • R-W 9:1. • Dry Feet. • 2 gulps-aid stn. Finding my groove. Focus out.

Course Details + Slices

Spectator Plan

Time Estimates

Process Goal

Swim	Bike	Run
	PART 2 • Same + Get to halfway. Focus in. Relax to EZ rhythm. Long freeway drive.	MILE 9-16 • Same + • Smile @ crowd • R-w 5:1 Cruising on a Sunday afternoon. Focus in.

Mental Strategies →

Transition Plan ↓

Meltdown Plan ↗

Swim	Bike	Run
	PART 3 • Same + • Stretch on 30's. Shift focus on 30. Best moments. ⋯▶ Batman music.	Glide up hill. McCormack QK. Battle. Party @ 13. MILE 17-END Same+ HR to 158. R-w 9:1/none. Stand up tall.
	PART 4 • Same + Spinning silk. Hum of the wheels. EZ on the legs. Cruising.	Fly downhill. Use bracelet for 7 mile by mile focus.
T1-walk. Long sleeves.	T2-Walk. C shorts.	(ER PLAN-Calm. Evaluate. Slow. Fuel. Recover. Continue)

10
RACE REPORT & POST RACE

The Race Report is a detailed recap of the day. The more detailed it is, the more helpful it will be in the future.
- How did it all turn out? Let your emotions flow along with the data.
- Relive your fine day.
- What did you do right and what did you do wrong? Learn from your experience for your next race.

Use your Race Plan as the basic structure of your report, but elaborate with specifics like weather, actual times and standing in your division, great moments and low points and of course, the finish.

Race reports can be shared with friends and family, or quietly stored in your Ironplanner. Write it a few days after the race but don't wait too long. Memories fade. If you had a bad day it is even more important to write about it. It will help put things in perspective and if nothing else, you can write it all down, then put it away and forget about it for awhile. If you are having a hard time, use the Race Report worksheet that is provided.

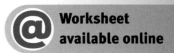
RACE REPORT WORKSHEET –

Here are some things to include in your race report.

Metrics
Name, date and location of race
High and low air temperature
Weather conditions
Water temperature
Swim time compared to expected & dream time
Rank in division and overall
Time/100 m
Transition 1 time
Bike time compared to expected & dream time
Splits
Rank in division and overall
Average cadence
Average speed
Transition 2 time
Run time compared to expected & dream time
Splits
Average pace/split
Rank in division and overall
Overall run pace
Total finish time compared to expected time
Heart Rate Average (by event or split

Evaluation of Race Plan

Overall was your Race Plan helpful?
How could it be improved?

Swim

Did your mental strategy help?
Which one helped the most?
Did you meet your process goals?

Transition 1

Did you meet your process goals?

Bike

Did your mental strategy help? How could it improve?
Which one helped the most?
Did your fueling strategy help? How could it improve?
Did you meet your process goals?
Did your choice of clothing work?
Did you use your special needs bag?

Transition 2

Did you meet your process goals?

Run

Did your mental strategy help? How could it improve?

Which strategy helped the most?

Did your fueling strategy help? How could it improve?

Did you meet your process goals?

Did your choice of clothing work?

Preparation

Did you have everything you needed in your race day bags? What was missing?

Was your mental preparation adequate? How could it improve?

Emotions

What were the emotional high points of the day? Describe them in detail.

What were the emotional low points of the day? Describe them in detail.

Are you satisfied with your emotional control during the race?

Recap of the day
Describe your wake-up routine and events up to arriving at the race venue...
Describe your feelings upon arrival at the race venue and while setting up your bike...
Describe the moments before the start...
Describe the swim...
Unusual sights/experiences during swim...
Exiting the water...
Transition 1...
Getting started on the bike...

The bike...
Unusual sights/experiences during bike leg...
Transition 2...
Starting the run...
The run...
Unusual sights/experiences during the run...
The finish...
The hours right after the finish...
The day after the race...
Will you do another Ironman...

POST-RACE

Life will be a celebration for several weeks after you become an Ironman. The first thought when you awaken each day will be your glorious accomplishment, followed by the realization that you don't have to train. You will make your social rounds, catching up with friends you neglected during training and retelling your story to anyone who will listen. You will proudly place symbols of your accomplishment on your car (stickers) and your body (maybe a tattoo, finisher jersey and hat).

At some point you will realize that the great adventure is behind you and you will feel a little lost. You will be relieved that the huge investment of time and energy paid off. You will be glad you are no longer a slave to your training schedule, but you will also miss the clarity of focus that has been drawing you towards race day for so many months.

You may not feel like setting any other goals for now. None would compare to what you just experienced. Still, you want to maintain your fitness to some degree and you have become addicted to training every day. So now what?

Having built a tremendous training base, consider what you would like to do with it. Maybe it would be fun to see what you could do in some short races. Perhaps you want to dust off the mountain bike or the trail running shoes and give them a whirl again. Maybe you really want to see where your cycling will take you if you work on speed for the rest of the year.

Get out there and start moving again when you are up to it. Resume maintenance level training until you get your sense of direction.

Set some small goals and make some plans on your Post Race worksheet. Be prepared to feel a little down, a little disoriented, a little uncertain for awhile. It will pass. You are and will always be an Ironman. Rejoice!

POST RACE WORKSHEET –

List at least 10 things you will do in the 30 days following your Ironman race.

1. _____

2. _____

3. _____

4. _____

5. _____

6. _____

7. _____

8. _____

9. _____

10. _____

11

IMPORTANT ODDS AND ENDS

SUPPLIES FOR YOUR CAR

When training for an Ironman, think of your car as a home away from home. A well-stocked vehicle will keep you comfortable after your sessions and will save you time.

1. Always have food in your car. Carry non-perishables like Ensure shakes, Zone or Power Bars, boxed juices. There will be times when you finish a workout and have to rush off to an appointment without time to eat. Refueling following workouts is imperative.

2. Having extra sets of swim and run gear in your car will allow you to take advantage of impromptu training opportunities. Keep a copy of your training plan available as well.

3. Minor medical/grooming challenges are easily handled with travel sized supplies. Carry Pepto Bismol, Aleve, Vaseline, Chap Stick, deodorant, breath mints, hairbrush, mouthwash, razor, lotion, and you are all set.

MAKE THE MOST OF TRANSITIONS

The transitions are very much part of your race so practice and plan them. Make sure you will have everything you need in your race day bags.

Most Ironman races have you place your transition items in bags, rather than spread on the ground near your bike. There are also changing tents with chairs inside and you are expected to sit and remove/put on your gear there, rather than outdoors.

SWIM TO BIKE TRANSITION

Keep your heart rate low during transition so you don't use precious energy. Considering that, there is little merit to racing through a transition. Walking will probably serve you better unless you are going for a time goal and every second counts. It takes a lot of discipline to walk into T1 (the swim to bike transition) because you are so full of energy and the crowd is cheering like mad. But patience rules the day so decide ahead of time what you will do and stick to your plan.

BIKE TO RUN TRANSITION

For athletes with flexible time goals, the bike to run transition is a brief time-out. By the time you go into that tent, the shine of the day has given way to the enormity of it. The task ahead is humbling and you see it on the faces of the other athletes. It is really the first time you see the faces without goggles, a helmet or sunglasses. The fatigue shows and in the brief glances and common suffering, there is kinship.

Transitions are an opportunity to cure whatever may be ailing you, at least for a few moments. Slowing down will allow your stomach to empty a little. At times the volunteers are so helpful they get in the way a little. This is another reason to have it clear in your own mind, precisely what you need to do while you are there.

BRICKS

Brick workouts help you tolerate running off the bike, but they also provide an opportunity to perfect your transition. Set up a simulated transition area and keep track of how long it takes to do the things you will do on race day like going to the bathroom and if applicable, changing clothes. On race day you will also be putting on a race number.

Make sure you have some fuel with you on the run in order to test your tolerances, especially after long rides. Even a 30 minute run after a long bike ride will tell you something about how you respond to various fuels late in the race.

SPECIAL CLOTHING CONSIDERATIONS

Ironman-distance races present unique challenges which require special clothing considerations. Changing clothes is an option in the transitions. There are advantages and disadvantages to changing clothes so you should consider the question carefully and experiment during training, especially when you are wet, hot and sticky and tired like you will be on race day.

Think twice about wearing a single piece triathlon suit for a race this long. Chances are you will be visiting the restroom sometime during the day and getting one of those suits off and on again when you are sticky and tired will slow you more than the aerodynamic benefit the suit provides.

SWIM

- Wear your wetsuit for a long (60 minute or more) swim at least once before race day. A short workout may not reveal the chaffing hot spots. On race day you will know where to apply anti-chaffing lotion such as Body Glide.

- If you put your swim cap over dry hair and don't submerge, your hair will stay nearly dry. If the weather is cold, dry hair will go a long way to keeping you from freezing to death on the bike.

- Take the time to dry off when it is cold out. Synthetic chamois-type towels are compact and will dry you quickly.

- If it is cold, consider putting dry clothes on after the swim. Practice this in training.

BIKE

- You will be spending lots of training time on the bike so you will need multiple sets of clothing for every kind of weather. The more clothing you have, the less time you will to spend looking around for what you need.

- Bike and Triathlon-specific clothing can be expensive so buy some of it on eBay.

- Since you will have the option of changing clothes in Transition 2 you don't have to run in the same shorts you wore on the bike. This gives you the option of wearing fully-padded cycling shorts.

- If it is hot, consider wearing a lightweight long-sleeved shirt on the bike. It can be a challenge to put on when you are wet but there are advantages:

  o You can stay very cool by dousing yourself with water and enjoying a new level of evaporative cooling.

  o You will not have to slather your arms and shoulders in sunscreen.

  o Being covered reduces the feeling of overexposure that comes with being out in the sun all day.

RUN

- Experiment with clothing during your long runs in hot weather. The clothes that feel great on a 30 minute run will not necessarily serve you well for many hours with moisture added.

- Water can cause blisters when it soaks your feet. Having dry socks can be very helpful so put them in your Bike to Run Bag #4, Run Special Needs #5 and in your Finish Line Bag #6.

- Experiment with compression shorts. If they fit snuggly enough, the support will feel great, especially after a long ride. If the seams are too rough, you will be in agony. Experiment.

- Plan for the worst. Hope for the best. Perhaps you look especially fetching in light blue shorts, but how will they look soaked in water and sweat after a few aid stations? Worse, what if an intestinal calamity befalls you? Basic black is the most forgiving color. Keep that in mind.

- If you wear a shirt with a pocket on race day, you can carry some small items that will make you more comfortable without having to pick-up your special needs bag. Smear some Vaseline and Chap Stick inside a plastic bag . Put some pain reliever, anti-inflammatories or Pepto Bismol in a piece of foil and viola, you have a mini medical station in your pocket.

- Races may require that you attach reflective tape to your running clothes. Small strips are available at vendors at the race venue, or you can buy it ahead of time. Remove it before the finish or your photo may be ruined by the light reflecting off the tape.

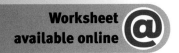
CONTACTS AND FACILITIES –

Keep important address and contact information here.

Name/Place & Phone#	E-mail & Address

Airline:

Bike transport:

Coach:

Hotel:

Lap Swim:
Alternative location:

Physical Therapist:

Bike Mechanic/Repair:

ABOUT THE AUTHOR

Photo by Dean Thomas

At 16, she became the first female ocean lifeguard in Laguna Beach, CA. Soon after, she became the first woman to row across the Channel from Catalina Island to Long Beach, CA. In college at the University of California Irvine, they did not have a women's rowing team in 1981, so she joined the men's team.

She became a lawyer and cheerfully gave up her law practice when her children were born. Her autistic daughter inspired her to co-author a ground breaking perspective on the subject. For sanity's sake she rediscovered her athletic roots and started running marathons and eventually triathlons. 3 years later she completed her first Ironman and wrote this book to help others organize their personal Ironman journey. Between Ironman races, she enjoys podium finishes in sprint and Olympic distance triathlons.

Visit her websites,
IngridLoosMiller.com, Shutdownsandstressinautism.com
and
Ironplanner.net.

PHOTO & ILLUSTRATION CREDITS

Cover photo:	Swim:	Sailfish
	Bike/Run:	Bakke Svensson/Ironman
Cover design:	Jens Vogelsang	

Photos on pages 38, 78, 133 by Henson-Roberts/Ironman
Photo on page 74 by Rich Cruse Photography-Ironman
All other photos by Bakke-Svensson/Ironman.

IRONMAN®-Edition

240 pages
Color-photo illustration throughout
Hardcover, 10" x 10"
ISBN 978-1-84126-114-0
$ 34.95 US
£ 24.95 UK/€ 29.95

128 pages
full-color print
30 photos
Paperback, 6 1/2" x 9 1/4"
ISBN: 978-1-84126-113-3
$ 16.95 US
£ 12.95 UK/€ 16.95

176 pages
full-color print
66 photos, 5 illustrations
Paperback, 6 1/2" x 9 1/4"
ISBN: 978-1-84126-111-9
$ 16.95 US
£ 12.95 UK/€ 16.95

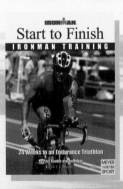

178 pages
full-color print
52 photos, 5 tables
Paperback, 5 3/4" x 8 1/4"
ISBN: 978-1-84126-102-7
$ 17.95 US
£ 12.95 UK/€ 16.90

Photo by Henson-Roberts/Ironman

www.m-m-sports.com

MEYER & MEYER SPORT

The Sports Publisher